**Fuzzy Friendships**

# Froggy Friends

## Written and illustrated by Lynne Davies

First published in 2023

Text © Lynne Davies
Illustration © Lynne Davies

The rights of Lynne Davies to be identified as the author and illustrator of this work has been asserted by them in accordance with the Copyright Designs and Patents Act 1988

All rights reserved

For my grandchildren Ben and Jennifer Wren

I like it when it's damp.
I like it when it's wet.
I like to hide amongst the leaves.
Oh I'm so glad we met.

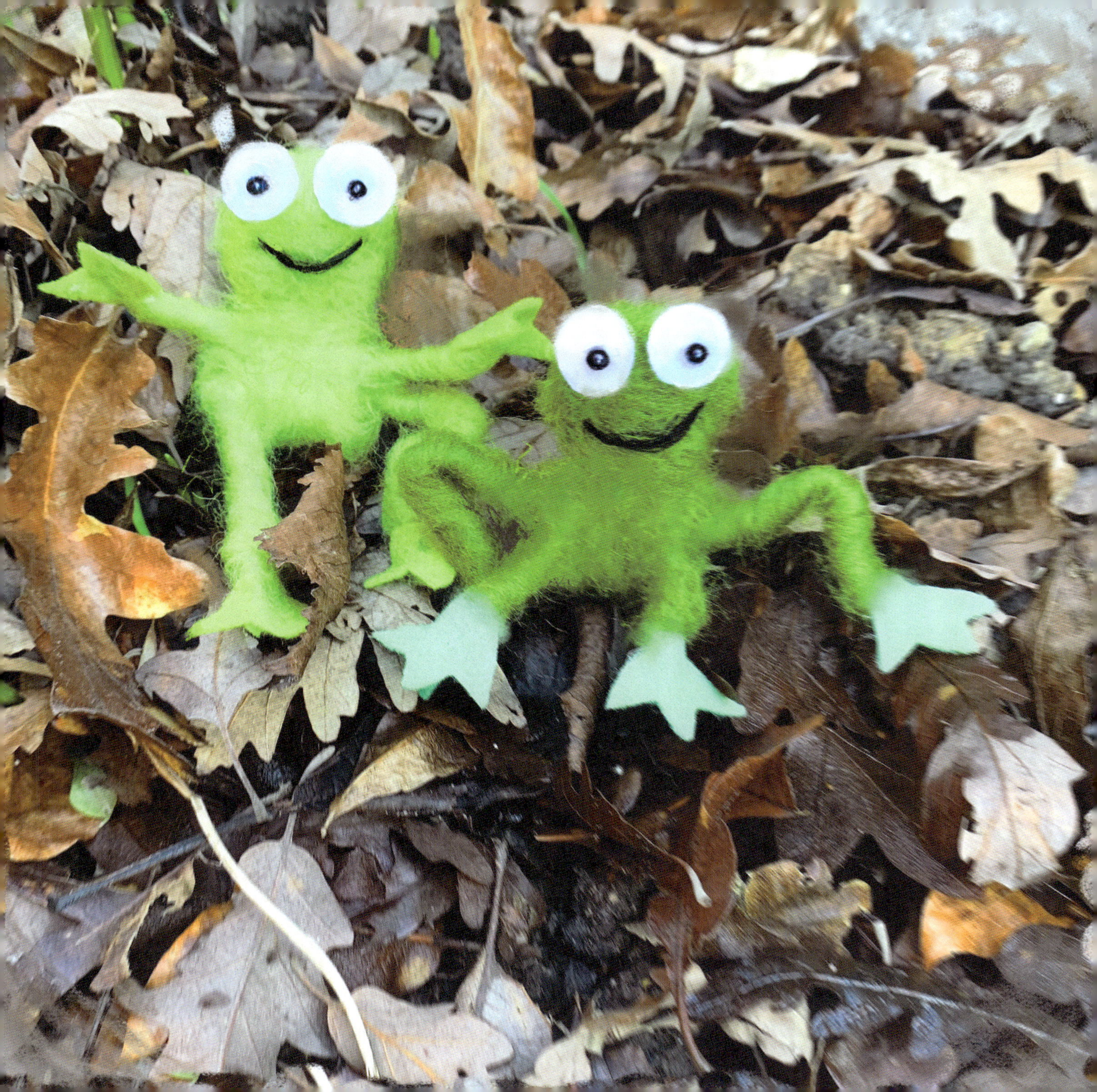

We can hide together and share some Froggy fun.
Maybe every now and then, enjoy a bit of sun!

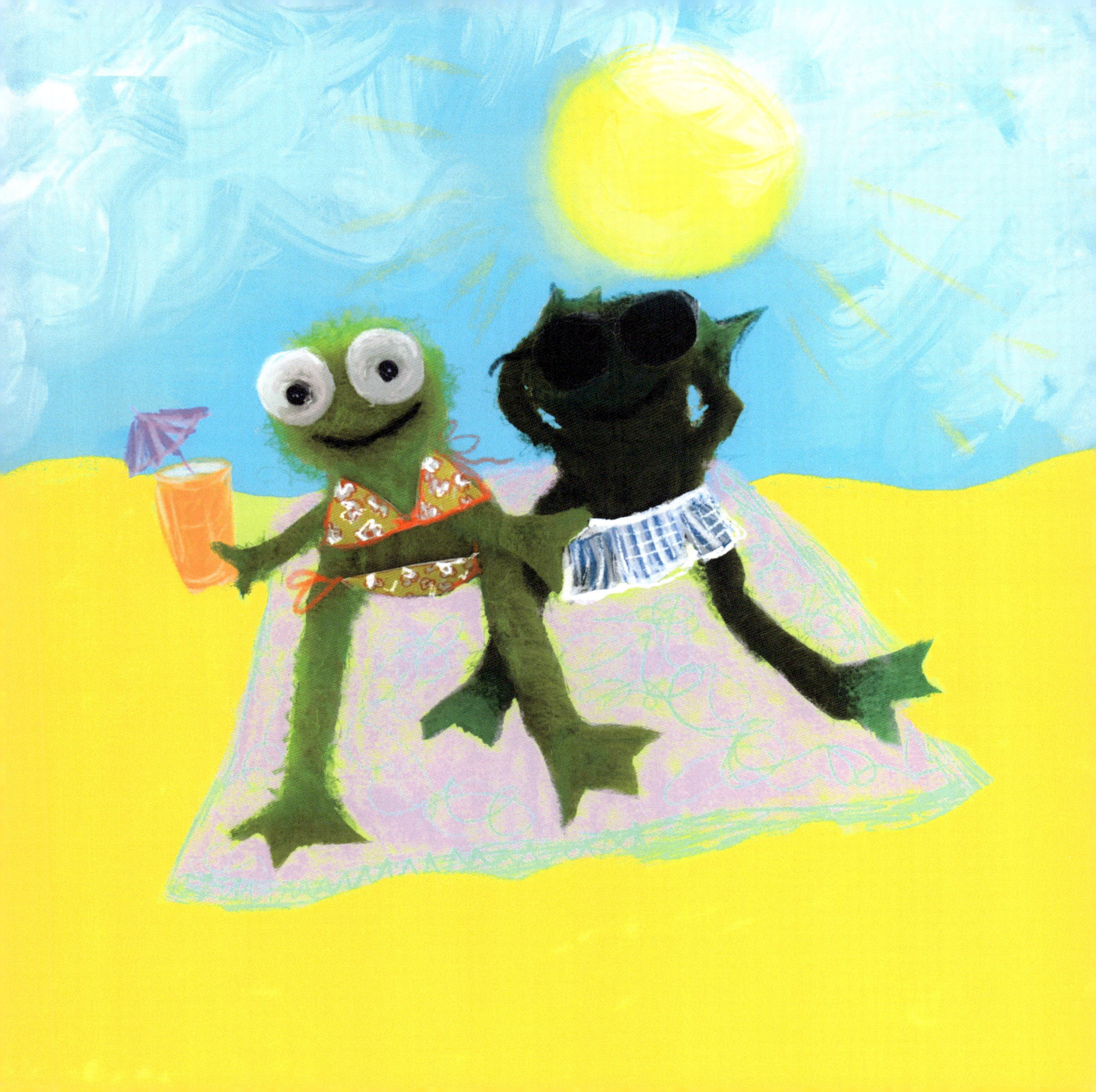

When it's really rainy,
We can leap in all the puddles.

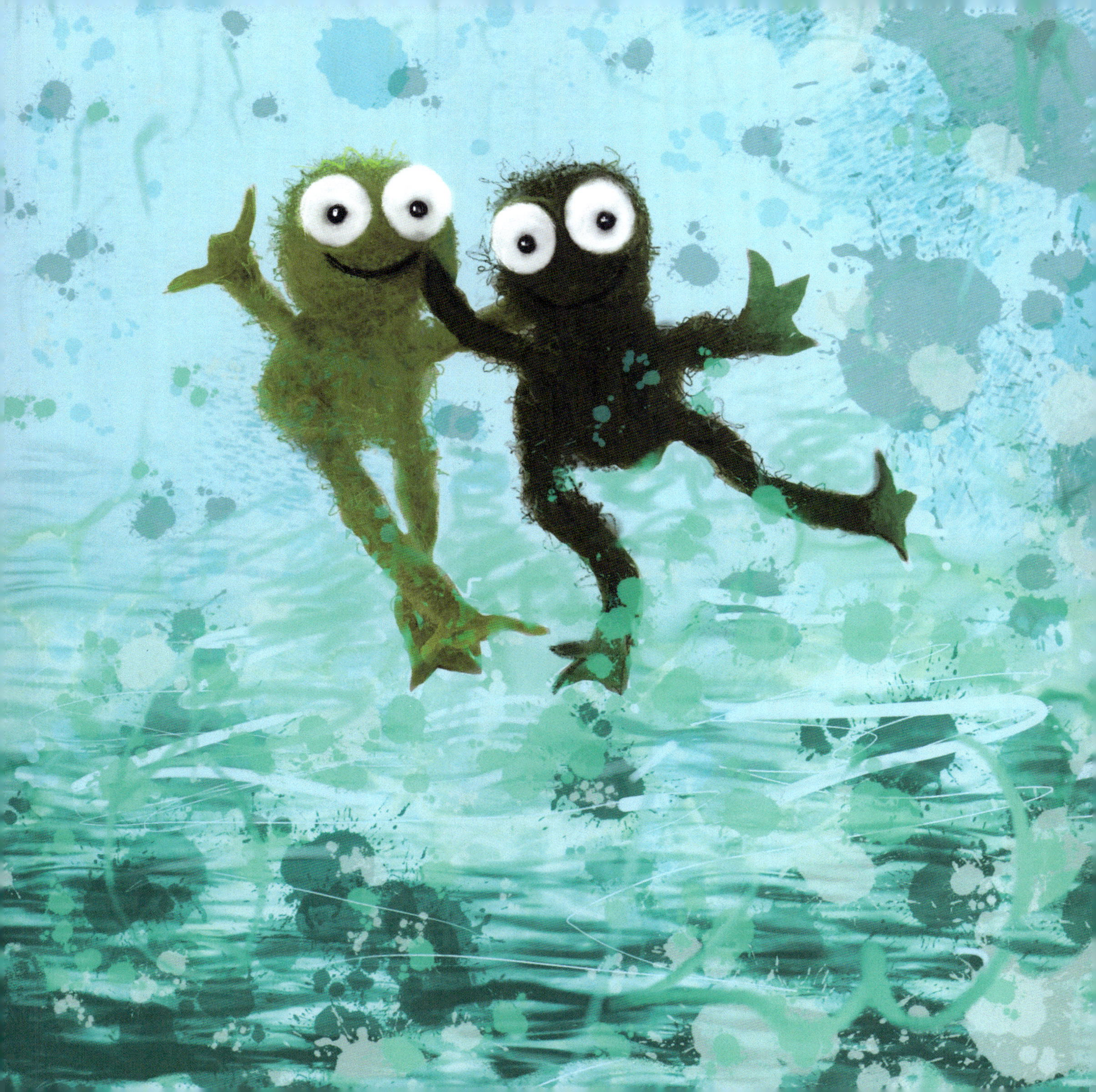

We'll croak and laugh
and muck about,
Then settle down for
cuddles.

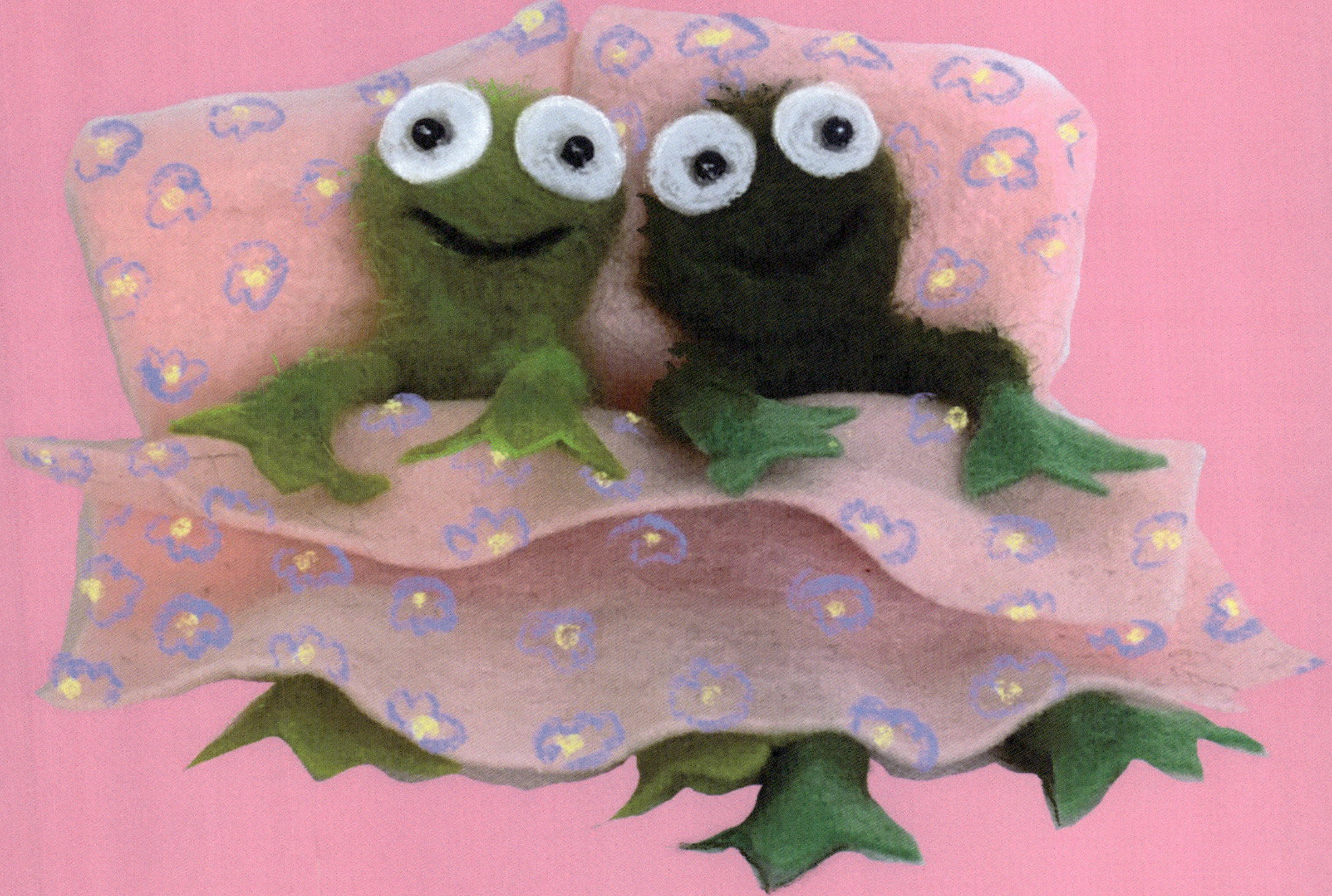

Life's a big adventure,
If you open your eyes wide.
Never mind the weather,
Get yourself outside!

FOOTPATH

We can sneak through people's gardens,
Especially when it's boggy.
Aren't we really lucky,
To live a life so Froggy.

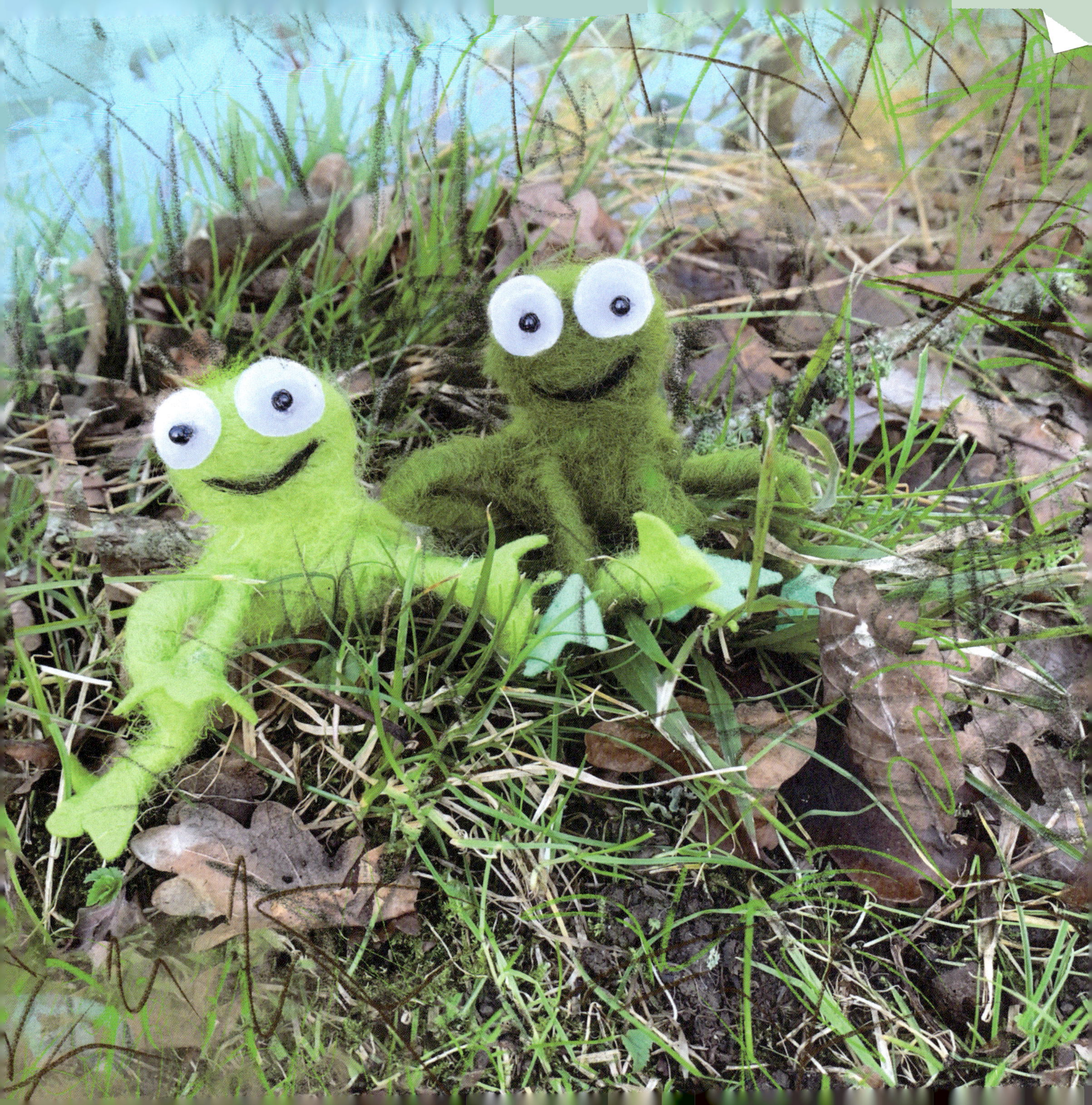

Come on, take a sneaky peak,There's sometimes holes in walls.

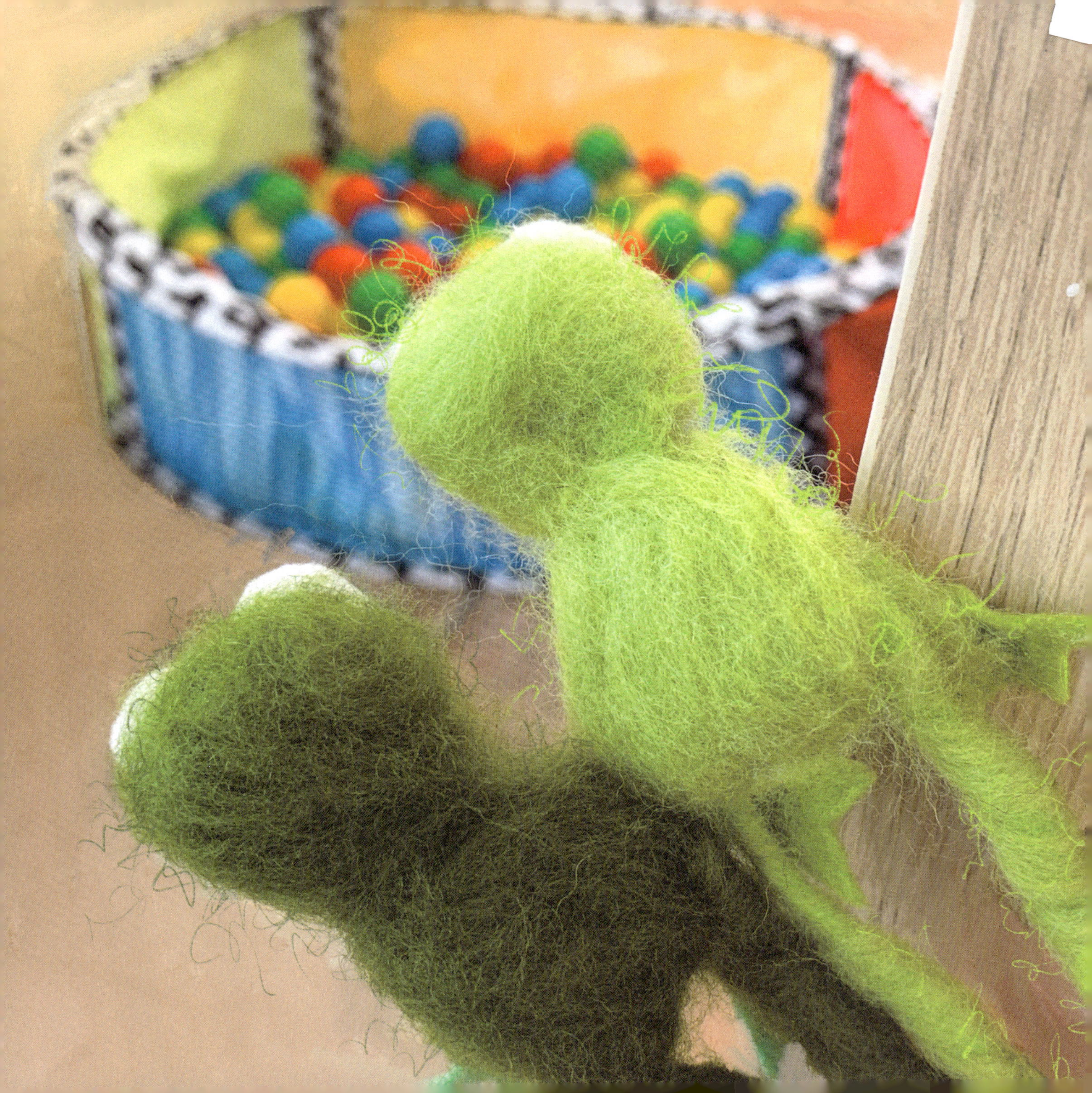

When we're absolutely sure it's clear
We can play amongst the balls!

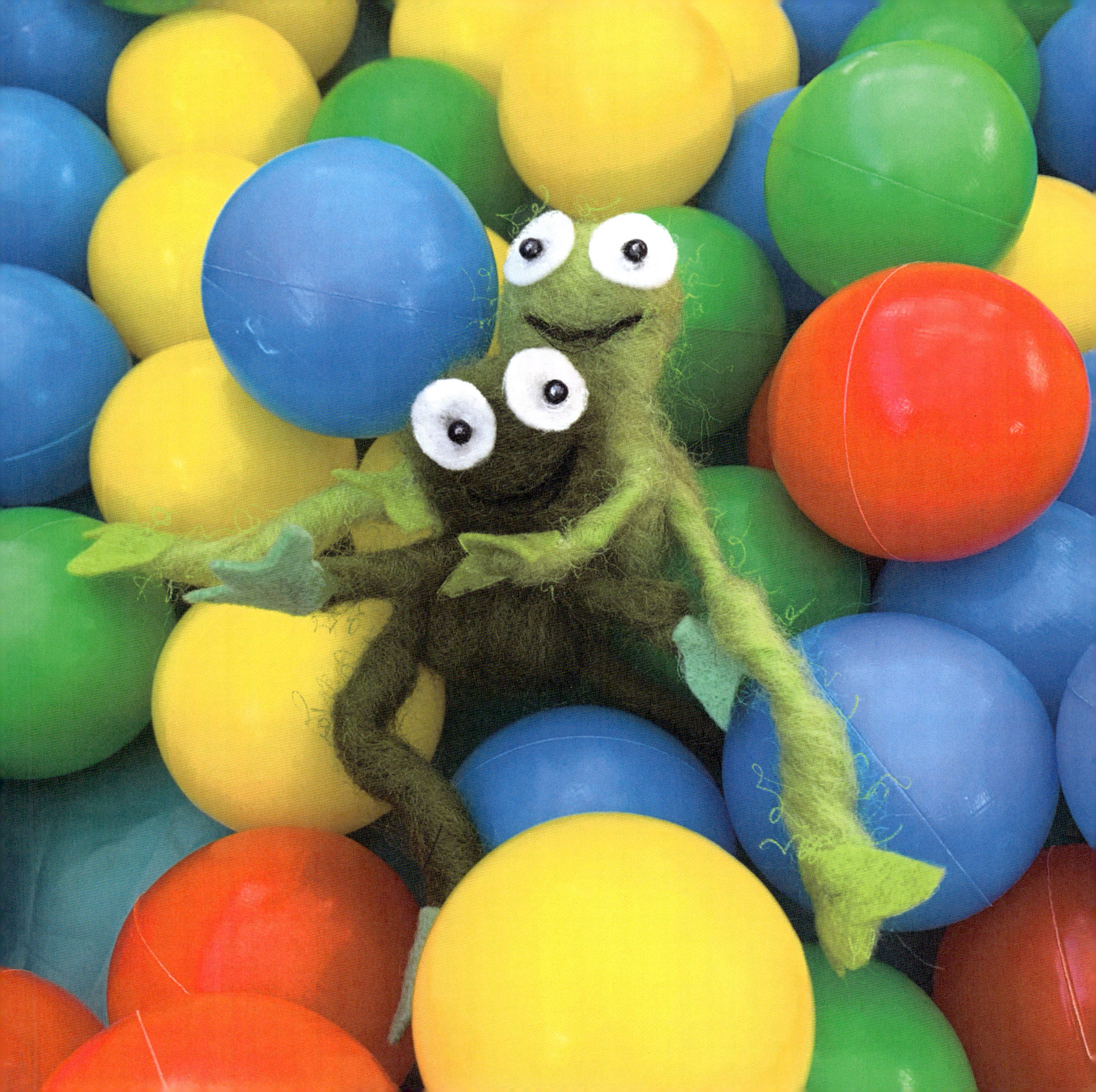

It's nice to have a Froggy friend,
Who cheers you up each day.
Do you have any Froggy friends?
Why not find one right away!

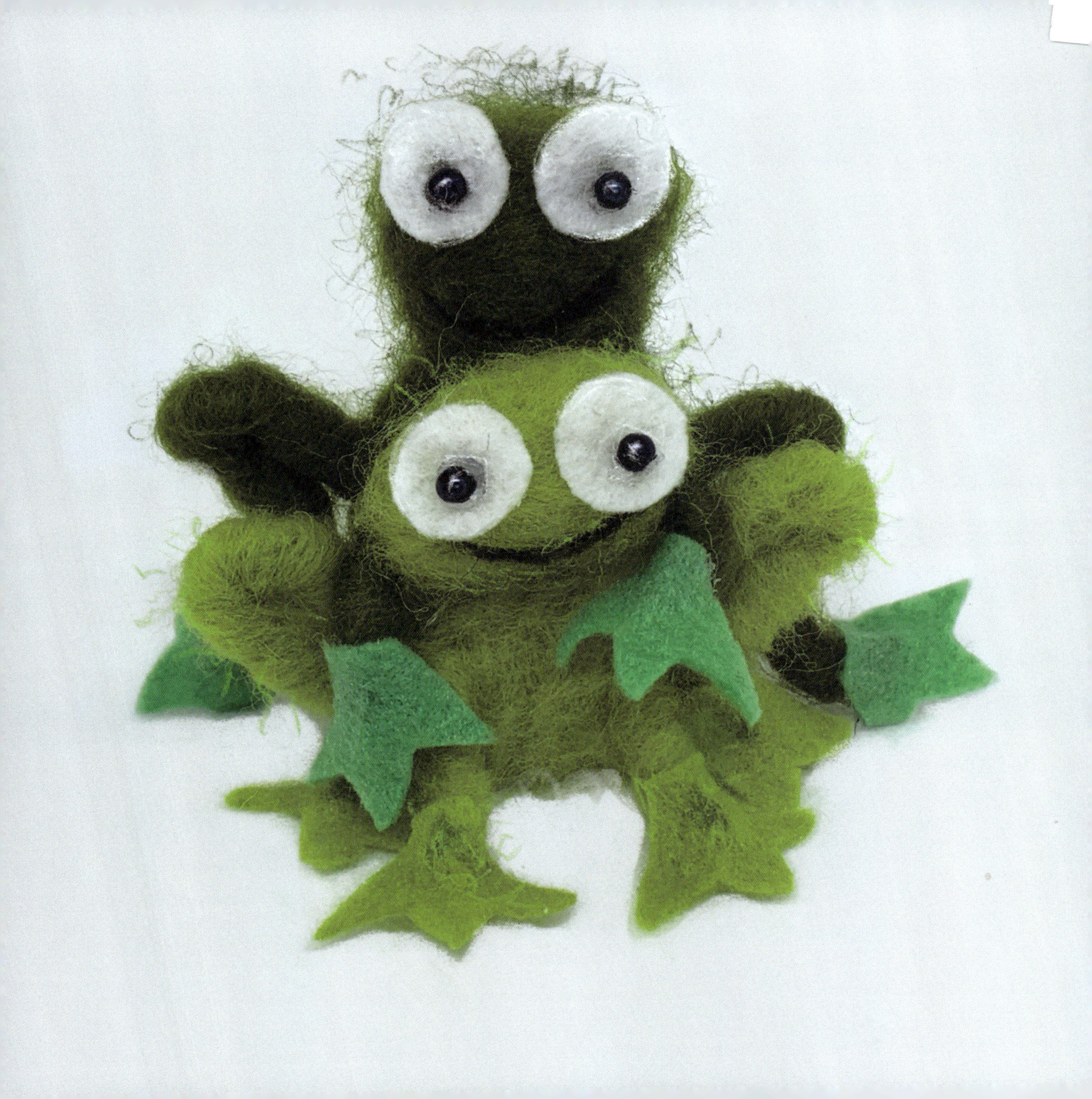

Further stories in this series on the way! Look out for…

The Foxy Four
Spikey's Feeling Naughty
Perfectly Puffin
Owly Feet
The Squee's hideaway

# About Lynne Davies

Lynne lives in Hampshire UK. A proud mum of three adult children and 'Gran Gran' of two.

An internationally acclaimed wildlife artist and nature lover who loves to create friendly, funny little characters in her spare time and write poems about them.

Lynne teaches art to children and she regularly tries out her new stories on her students. Their delighted response encouraged her to publish to a wider audience.

# Awards

BBC Wildlife Artist of the Year finalist
David Shepherd Wildlife Artist of the Year Finalist
SAA Artist of the Year Finalist
TWASI Gold medal winner

Check out Lynne Davies Art at lynnedavies.com

# Fuzzy Friendships

Printed in Great Britain
by Amazon